# Yeah, I Know "Write"

## Freestyle Writing & Note-Taking Composition

## Alicia "WATERS"

Yeah, I Know "Write"

For ordering, booking, permission, or questions, contact the author.
www.amazon.com/author/alicianwaters
www.anwempires@gmail.com

ISBN:9781077401730


Printed in the United States of America by Kindle Direct Publishing

# Yeah, I Know "Write"

# Note-Taking Space

## Yeah, I Know "Write"

# Note-Taking Space

Yeah, I Know "Write"

# Note-Taking Space

Yeah, I Know "Write"

# Note-Taking Space

Yeah, I Know "Write"

# Note-Taking Space

Yeah, I Know "Write"

# Note-Taking Space

## Yeah, I Know "Write"

# Note-Taking Space

Yeah, I Know "Write"

# Note-Taking Space

Yeah, I Know "Write"

# Note-Taking Space

Yeah, I Know "Write"

# Note-Taking Space

Yeah, I Know "Write"

# Note-Taking Space

Yeah, I Know "Write"

# Note-Taking Space

Yeah, I Know "Write"

# Note-Taking Space

Yeah, I Know "Write"

# Note-Taking Space

Yeah, I Know "Write"

# Note-Taking Space

Yeah, I Know "Write"

# Note-Taking Space

Yeah, I Know "Write"

# Note-Taking Space

Yeah, I Know "Write"

# Note-Taking Space

Yeah, I Know "Write"

# Note-Taking Space

Yeah, I Know "Write"

# Note-Taking Space

Yeah, I Know "Write"

# Note-Taking Space

Yeah, I Know "Write"

# Note-Taking Space

Yeah, I Know "Write"

# Note-Taking Space

Yeah, I Know "Write"

# Note-Taking Space

Yeah, I Know "Write"

# Note-Taking Space

Yeah, I Know "Write"

# Note-Taking Space

Yeah, I Know "Write"

# Note-Taking Space

Yeah, I Know "Write"

# Note-Taking Space

Yeah, I Know "Write"

# Note-Taking Space

Yeah, I Know "Write"

# Note-Taking Space

Yeah, I Know "Write"

# Note-Taking Space

Yeah, I Know "Write"

# Note-Taking Space

Yeah, I Know "Write"

# Note-Taking Space

Yeah, I Know "Write"

# Note-Taking Space

Yeah, I Know "Write"

# Note-Taking Space

Yeah, I Know "Write"

# Note-Taking Space

Yeah, I Know "Write"

# Note-Taking Space

Yeah, I Know "Write"

# Note-Taking Space

Yeah, I Know "Write"

# Note-Taking Space

Yeah, I Know "Write"

# Note-Taking Space

Yeah, I Know "Write"

# Note-Taking Space

Yeah, I Know "Write"

# Note-Taking Space

Yeah, I Know "Write"

# Note-Taking Space

Yeah, I Know "Write"

# Note-Taking Space

Yeah, I Know "Write"

# Note-Taking Space

Yeah, I Know "Write"

# Note-Taking Space

Yeah, I Know "Write"

# Note-Taking Space

Yeah, I Know "Write"

# Note-Taking Space

Yeah, I Know "Write"

# Note-Taking Space

Yeah, I Know "Write"

# Note-Taking Space

Yeah, I Know "Write"

# Note-Taking Space

Yeah, I Know "Write"

# Note-Taking Space

Yeah, I Know "Write"

# Note-Taking Space

Yeah, I Know "Write"

# Note-Taking Space

Yeah, I Know "Write"

# Note-Taking Space

Yeah, I Know "Write"

# Note-Taking Space

Yeah, I Know "Write"

# Note-Taking Space

Yeah, I Know "Write"

# Note-Taking Space

Yeah, I Know "Write"

# Note-Taking Space

Yeah, I Know "Write"

# Note-Taking Space

Yeah, I Know "Write"

# Note-Taking Space

Yeah, I Know "Write"

# Note-Taking Space

Yeah, I Know "Write"

# Note-Taking Space

Yeah, I Know "Write"

# Note-Taking Space

Yeah, I Know "Write"

# Note-Taking Space

Yeah, I Know "Write"

# Note-Taking Space

Yeah, I Know "Write"

# Note-Taking Space

Yeah, I Know "Write"

# Note-Taking Space

Yeah, I Know "Write"

# Note-Taking Space

Yeah, I Know "Write"

# Note-Taking Space

Yeah, I Know "Write"

# Note-Taking Space

Yeah, I Know "Write"

# Note-Taking Space

Yeah, I Know "Write"

# Note-Taking Space

Yeah, I Know "Write"

# Note-Taking Space

Yeah, I Know "Write"

# Note-Taking Space

Yeah, I Know "Write"

# Note-Taking Space

Yeah, I Know "Write"

# Note-Taking Space

Yeah, I Know "Write"

# Note-Taking Space

Yeah, I Know "Write"

# Note-Taking Space

Yeah, I Know "Write"

# Note-Taking Space

Yeah, I Know "Write"

# Note-Taking Space

Yeah, I Know "Write"

# Note-Taking Space

Yeah, I Know "Write"

# Note-Taking Space

Yeah, I Know "Write"

# Note-Taking Space

Yeah, I Know "Write"

# Note-Taking Space

Yeah, I Know "Write"

# Note-Taking Space

Yeah, I Know "Write"

# Note-Taking Space

Yeah, I Know "Write"

# Note-Taking Space

Yeah, I Know "Write"

# Note-Taking Space

Yeah, I Know "Write"

# Note-Taking Space

Yeah, I Know "Write"

# Note-Taking Space

Yeah, I Know "Write"

# Note-Taking Space

Yeah, I Know "Write"

# Note-Taking Space

Yeah, I Know "Write"

# Note-Taking Space

Yeah, I Know "Write"

# Note-Taking Space

Yeah, I Know "Write"

# Note-Taking Space

Yeah, I Know "Write"

# Note-Taking Space

Yeah, I Know "Write"

# Related Resources on Amazon

Noteworthy: (Freestyle Writing & Note Taking Composition)

Got Calls? (Conference Calls Note-Taking Composition)

## Visit the Author's Amazon Page
www.amazon.com/author/alicianwaters

## To Book the Author for
## Speaking Engagements
Email: anwempires@gmail.com

If you enjoyed this resource, please feel free to leave a positive review on Amazon.

## Thanks & Blessings

Yeah, I Know "Write"